The Gospel of Mark

Colouring Book

The Soothing, Simple to Colour Words of the Bible

ESTHER PINCINI

The Gospel of Mark Colouring Book
The Soothing, Simple to Colour Words of the Bible

by Esther Pincini

Includes the complete text of the Gospel of Mark from
the King James Version Bible, Cambridge Edition, translated
from the original tongues and appointed to be read in Churches.

Copyright © Magdalene Press 2016

ISBN 978-1-77335-102-5

No part of this publication may be reproduced, stored in a retrieval system, or transmitted in any form or by any means, electronic, mechanical, photocopying, recording or otherwise without written permission of the publisher.

Magdalene Press, 2016

The Gospel According to St. Mark

CHAPTER 1

THE beginning of the gospel of Jesus Christ, the Son of God;

2 As it is written

in the prophets, Behold, I send my messenger before thy face, which shall prepare thy way before thee.

3 The voice of

one crying in the wilderness, Prepare ye the way of the Lord, make his paths straight.

4 John did baptize in the

wilderness, and preach the baptism of repentance for the remission of sins.

5 And there went out unto

him all the land
of Judæa, and
they of
Jerusalem, and
were all baptized
of him in the
river of Jordan,
confessing their

sins.

6 And John was clothed with camel's hair, and with a girdle of a skin about his loins; and he did eat locusts and

wild honey;
7 And preached, saying, There cometh one mightier than I after me, the latchet of whose shoes I am not

worthy to stoop down and unloose.

8 I indeed have baptized you with water: but he shall baptize you with the

Holy Ghost.

9 And it came to pass in those days, that Jesus came from Nazareth of Galilee, and was baptized of John

in Jordan.
10 And straightway coming up out of the water, he saw the heavens opened, and the Spirit like a dove

descending upon him:

11 And there came a voice from heaven, *saying*, Thou art my beloved Son, in whom I am

well pleased.

12 And immediately the Spirit driveth him into the wilderness.

13 And he was there in the

wilderness forty days, tempted of Satan; and was with the wild beasts; and the angels ministered unto him.

14 Now after

that John was put in prison, Jesus came into Galilee, preaching the gospel of the kingdom of God,

15 And saying, The time is fulfilled, and the kingdom of God is at hand: repent ye, and believe the gospel.

16 Now as he

walked by the sea of Galilee, he saw Simon and Andrew his brother casting a net into the sea: for they were fishers.

17 And Jesus said unto them, Come ye after me, and I will make you to become fishers of men.

18 And

straightway they forsook their nets, and followed him.

19 And when he had gone a little further thence, he saw James the

son of Zebedee, and John his brother, who also were in the ship mending their nets.

20 And straightway he

called them: and they left their father Zebedee in the ship with the hired servants, and went after him.
21 And they

went into Capernaum; and straightway on the sabbath day he entered into the synagogue, and taught.

22 And they

were astonished at his doctrine: for he taught them as one that had authority, and not as the scribes.

23 And there

was in their synagogue a man with an unclean spirit; and he cried out,

24 Saying, Let *us* alone; what have we to do with

thee, thou Jesus of Nazareth? art thou come to destroy us? I know thee who thou art, the Holy One of God.

25 And Jesus rebuked him, saying, Hold thy peace, and come out of him.

26 And when the unclean spirit had torn him,

and cried with a loud voice, he came out of him. 27 And they were all amazed, insomuch that they questioned among themselves, saying, What thing is this? what new doctrine *is* this? for with authority commandeth he even the unclean spirits, and they do obey him.

28 And immediately his fame spread abroad throughout all

the region round about Galilee. 29 And forthwith, when they were come out of the synagogue, they entered into the house of Simon and Andrew, with James and John.

30 But Simon's wife's mother lay sick of a fever, and anon they

tell him of her. 31 And he came and took her by the hand, and lifted her up; and immediately the fever left her, and she ministered unto them.

32 And at even, when the sun did set, they brought unto him all that were diseased, and them that

were possessed with devils.

33 And all the city was gathered together at the door.

34 And he healed many that

were sick of divers diseases, and cast out many devils; and suffered not the devils to speak, because they knew him.

35 And in the morning, rising up a great while before day, he went out, and departed into a solitary place, and there prayed.

36 And Simon and they that were with him followed after him.

37 And when they had found him, they said

unto him, All *men* seek for thee.

38 And he said unto them, Let us go into the next towns, that I may preach

there also: for therefore came I forth.

39 And he preached in their synagogues throughout all Galilee, and cast

out devils.

40 And there came a leper to him, beseeching him, and kneeling down to him, and saying unto him,

If thou wilt, thou canst make me clean.

41 And Jesus, moved with compassion, put forth *his* hand, and touched

him, and saith unto him, I will; be thou clean.

42 And as soon as he had spoken, immediately the leprosy departed

from him, and he was cleansed. 43 And he straitly charged him, and forthwith sent him away; 44 And saith unto him, See thou say nothing to any man: but go thy way, shew thyself to the priest, and offer for thy cleansing those things which Moses commanded, for a testimony unto them.

45 But he went out, and began to publish *it* much, and to

blaze abroad the matter, insomuch that Jesus could no more openly enter into the city, but was without in desert places: and they came to him from every quarter.

CHAPTER 2

AND again he

entered into Capernaum, after *some* days; and it was noised that he was in the house.

2 And straightway

many were
gathered
together,
insomuch that
there was no
room to receive
them, no, not so
much as about

the door: and he preached the word unto them.

3 And they come unto him, bringing one sick of the palsy, which was borne

of four.
 4 And when they could not come nigh unto him for the press, they uncovered the roof where he

was: and when they had broken *it* up, they let down the bed wherein the sick of the palsy lay. 5 When Jesus saw their faith, he said unto the sick of the palsy, Son, thy sins be forgiven thee.

6 But there were certain of the scribes sitting there, and

reasoning in their hearts, 7 Why doth this *man* thus speak blasphemies? who can forgive sins but God only?

8 And immediately when Jesus perceived in his spirit that they so reasoned within themselves, he

said unto them, Why reason ye these things in your hearts?

9 Whether is it easier to say to the sick of the palsy, *Thy* sins be

forgiven thee; or to say, Arise, and take up thy bed, and walk?

10 But that ye may know that the Son of man hath power on

earth to forgive sins, (he saith to the sick of the palsy,)

11 I say unto thee, Arise, and take up thy bed, and go thy way

into thine house. 12 And immediately he arose, took up the bed, and went forth before them all; insomuch that they were all amazed, and glorified God, saying, We never saw it on this fashion.

13 And he went forth again by

the sea side; and all the multitude resorted unto him, and he taught them.

14 And as he passed by, he saw Levi the *son*

of Alphæus sitting at the receipt of custom, and said unto him, Follow me. And he arose and followed him.

15 And it came to pass, that, as Jesus sat at meat in his house, many publicans and sinners sat also together with Jesus and

his disciples: for there were many, and they followed him.

16 And when the scribes and Pharisees saw him eat with

publicans and sinners, they said unto his disciples, How is it that he eateth and drinketh with publicans and sinners?

17 When Jesus heard *it*, he saith unto them, They that are whole have no need of the physician, but they that are sick: I came not

to call the righteous, but sinners to repentance.

18 And the disciples of John and of the Pharisees used to

fast: and they come and say unto him, Why do the disciples of John and of the Pharisees fast, but thy disciples fast not?

19 And Jesus said unto them, Can the children of the bridechamber fast, while the bridegroom is

with them? as long as they have the bridegroom with them, they cannot fast.

20 But the days will come, when the bridegroom

shall be taken away from them, and then shall they fast in those days.

21 No man also seweth a piece of new cloth on an

old garment: else the new piece that filled it up taketh away from the old, and the rent is made worse.

22 And no man

putteth new wine into old bottles: else the new wine doth burst the bottles, and the wine is spilled, and the bottles will be marred: but new wine must be put into new bottles.

23 And it came to pass, that he went through the corn fields on

the sabbath day; and his disciples began, as they went, to pluck the ears of corn. 24 And the Pharisees said unto him,

Behold, why do they on the sabbath day that which is not lawful?

25 And he said unto them, Have ye never read

what David did, when he had need, and was an hungred, he, and they that were with him?

26 How he went into the house of

God in the days of Abiathar the high priest, and did eat the shewbread, which is not lawful to eat but for the priests, and gave also to them which were with him?

27 And he said unto them, The sabbath was made for man, and not man for

the sabbath:
28 Therefore the Son of man is Lord also of the sabbath.

CHAPTER 3

AND he entered again into the synagogue; and there was a man there which had a withered hand. 2 And they watched him, whether he would heal him on the sabbath day; that they might accuse him.

3 And he saith

unto the man which had the withered hand, Stand forth.

4 And he saith unto them, Is it lawful to do good on the

sabbath days, or to do evil? to save life, or to kill? But they held their peace.

5 And when he had looked round about on

them with anger, being grieved for the hardness of their hearts, he saith unto the man, Stretch forth thine hand. And he stretched *it* out: and his hand was restored whole as the other.

6 And the Pharisees went forth, and straightway took

counsel with the Herodians against him, how they might destroy him. 7 But Jesus withdrew himself with his disciples to the sea: and a great multitude from Galilee followed him, and from Judæa,

8 And from Jerusalem, and

from Idumæa, and *from* beyond Jordan; and they about Tyre and Sidon, a great multitude, when they had heard what great things he did, came unto him.

9 And he spake to his disciples, that a small ship should wait on him because of the multitude,

lest they should throng him.

10 For he had healed many; insomuch that they pressed upon him for to touch him, as

many as had plagues.

11 And unclean spirits, when they saw him, fell down before him, and cried, saying, Thou art

the Son of God.
12 And he straitly charged them that they should not make him known.
13 And he goeth up into a

mountain, and calleth *unto him* whom he would: and they came unto him.

14 And he ordained twelve, that they should

be with him, and that he might send them forth to preach,

15 And to have power to heal sicknesses, and to cast out

devils:

16 And Simon he surnamed Peter;

17 And James the *son* of Zebedee, and John the brother

of James; and he surnamed them Boanerges, which is, The sons of thunder:
18 And Andrew, and Philip, and

Bartholomew, and Matthew, and Thomas, and James the *son* of Alphæus, and Thaddæus, and Simon the Canaanite,

19 And Judas Iscariot, which also betrayed him: and they went into an house.

20 And the multitude

cometh together again, so that they could not so much as eat bread.

21 And when his friends heard *of it*, they went

out to lay hold on him: for they said, He is beside himself.

22 And the scribes which came down from Jerusalem said,

He hath Beelzebub, and by the prince of the devils casteth he out devils.

23 And he called them *unto him*, and said

unto them in parables, How can Satan cast out Satan?

24 And if a kingdom be divided against itself, that

kingdom cannot stand.

25 And if a house be divided against itself, that house cannot stand.

26 And if Satan

rise up against himself, and be divided, he cannot stand, but hath an end. 27 No man can enter into a strong man's house, and spoil his goods, except he will first bind the strong man; and then he will spoil his house.

28 Verily I say unto you, All

sins shall be forgiven unto the sons of men, and blasphemies wherewith soever they shall blaspheme:

29 But he that

shall blaspheme against the Holy Ghost hath never forgiveness, but is in danger of eternal damnation:

30 Because they said, He hath an unclean spirit.

31 There came then his brethren and his mother, and, standing without, sent

unto him, calling him.

32 And the multitude sat about him, and they said unto him, Behold, thy mother and thy

brethren without seek for thee.

33 And he answered them, saying, Who is my mother, or my brethren?

34 And he

looked round about on them which sat about him, and said, Behold my mother and my brethren!

35 For

whosoever shall do the will of God, the same is my brother, and my sister, and mother.

CHAPTER 4

AND he began again to teach by the sea side: and there was gathered unto him a great multitude, so that he entered into a ship, and sat in the sea; and the whole multitude was by the sea on the land.

2 And he taught them many

things by parables, and said unto them in his doctrine, 3 Hearken; Behold, there went out a sower to sow:

4 And it came to pass, as he sowed, some fell by the way side, and the fowls of the air came and devoured it up.
5 And some fell

on stony ground, where it had not much earth; and immediately it sprang up, because it had no depth of earth:

6 But when the sun was up, it was scorched; and because it had no root, it withered away.

7 And some fell among thorns,

and the thorns grew up, and choked it, and it yielded no fruit. 8 And other fell on good ground, and did yield fruit that sprang up and increased; and brought forth, some thirty, and some sixty, and some an hundred.

9 And he said

unto them, He that hath ears to hear, let him hear.

10 And when he was alone, they that were about him with the

twelve asked of him the parable. 11 And he said unto them, Unto you it is given to know the mystery of the kingdom of

God: but unto them that are without, all *these* things are done in parables:

12 That seeing they may see, and not perceive;

and hearing they may hear, and not understand; lest at any time they should be converted, and *their* sins should be forgiven them.

13 And he said unto them, Know ye not this parable? and how then will ye know all parables?

14 The sower soweth the word.

15 And these are they by the way side, where the word is sown; but when

they have heard, Satan cometh immediately, and taketh away the word that was sown in their hearts.

16 And these

are they likewise which are sown on stony ground; who, when they have heard the word, immediately receive it with

gladness;
 17 And have no root in themselves, and so endure but for a time: afterward, when affliction or

persecution ariseth for the word's sake, immediately they are offended.

18 And these are they which are sown among

thorns; such as hear the word, 19 And the cares of this world, and the deceitfulness of riches, and the lusts of other things entering in, choke the word, and it becometh unfruitful.

20 And these are they which are sown on

good ground; such as hear the word, and receive *it*, and bring forth fruit, some thirtyfold, some sixty, and some an hundred.

21 And he said unto them, Is a candle brought to be put under a bushel, or under a bed? and not to be set on a

candlestick? 22 For there is nothing hid, which shall not be manifested; neither was any thing kept secret, but that it should come abroad.

23 If any man have ears to hear, let him hear.

24 And he said unto them, Take heed what ye

hear: with what measure ye mete, it shall be measured to you: and unto you that hear shall more be given.
25 For he that

hath, to him shall be given: and he that hath not, from him shall be taken even that which he hath.

26 And he said,

So is the kingdom of God, as if a man should cast seed into the ground; 27 And should sleep, and rise night and day, and the seed should spring and grow up, he knoweth not how.

28 For the earth bringeth forth fruit of herself;

first the blade, then the ear, after that the full corn in the ear.
29 But when the fruit is brought forth, immediately he

putteth in the sickle, because the harvest is come.

30 And he said, Whereunto shall we liken the kingdom of

God? or with what comparison shall we compare it?

31 *It is* like a grain of mustard seed, which, when it is sown

in the earth, is less than all the seeds that be in the earth:

32 But when it is sown, it groweth up, and becometh

greater than all herbs, and shooteth out great branches; so that the fowls of the air may lodge under the shadow of it.

33 And with many such parables spake he the word unto them, as they were able to hear *it*.

34 But without

a parable spake he not unto them: and when they were alone, he expounded all things to his disciples.

35 And the

same day, when the even was come, he saith unto them, Let us pass over unto the other side.

36 And when

they had sent away the multitude, they took him even as he was in the ship. And there were also with him other little

ships.
 37 And there arose a great storm of wind, and the waves beat into the ship, so that it was now full.

38 And he was in the hinder part of the ship, asleep on a pillow: and they awake him, and say unto him, Master, carest

thou not that we perish? 39 And he arose, and rebuked the wind, and said unto the sea, Peace, be still.

And the wind ceased, and there was a great calm. 40 And he said unto them, Why are ye so fearful? how is it that ye have no faith?

41 And they feared exceedingly, and said one to another, What manner of man is this, that even the wind and the

sea obey him?

HAPTER 5

AND they came over unto the other side of the sea, into the

country of the Gadarenes.

2 And when he was come out of the ship, immediately there met him out of the tombs

a man with an unclean spirit, 3 Who had *his* dwelling among the tombs; and no man could bind him, no, not with chains:

4 Because that he had been often bound with fetters and chains, and the chains had been plucked asunder by him, and the

fetters broken in pieces: neither could any *man* tame him.

5 And always, night and day, he was in the mountains, and

in the tombs, crying, and cutting himself with stones.

6 But when he saw Jesus afar off, he ran and worshipped him,

7 And cried with a loud voice, and said, What have I to do with thee, Jesus, *thou* Son of the most high God? I adjure

thee by God, that thou torment me not. 8 For he said unto him, Come out of the man, *thou* unclean spirit.

9 And he asked him, What *is* thy name? And he answered, saying, My name *is* Legion: for we are many.

10 And he

besought him much that he would not send them away out of the country. 11 Now there was there nigh unto the mountains a great herd of swine feeding. 12 And all the devils besought him, saying, Send us into the swine, that we

may enter into them.
 13 And forthwith Jesus gave them leave. And the unclean spirits went out, and entered into

the swine: and the herd ran violently down a steep place into the sea, (they were about two thousand;) and were choked in the sea.

14 And they that fed the swine fled, and told *it* in the city, and in the country. And they went out to

see what it was that was done. 15 And they come to Jesus, and see him that was possessed with the devil, and had the legion, sitting, and clothed, and in his right mind: and they were afraid.

16 And they that saw *it* told them how it

befell to him that was possessed with the devil, and *also* concerning the swine.

17 And they began to pray

him to depart out of their coasts.

18 And when he was come into the ship, he that had been possessed with

the devil prayed him that he might be with him.

19 Howbeit Jesus suffered him not, but saith unto him,

Go home to thy friends, and tell them how great things the Lord hath done for thee, and hath had compassion on thee.

20 And he departed, and began to publish in Decapolis how great things Jesus had done for him: and all *men* did marvel.

21 And when Jesus was passed over again by ship unto the other side, much people gathered unto him: and he was nigh unto

the sea.

22 And, behold, there cometh one of the rulers of the synagogue, Jairus by name; and when he saw

him, he fell at his feet,
 23 And besought him greatly, saying, My little daughter lieth at the point of

death: *I pray thee,* come and lay thy hands on her, that she may be healed; and she shall live.

24 And *Jesus* went with him;

and much people followed him, and thronged him.

25 And a certain woman, which had an issue of blood twelve

years,
26 And had suffered many things of many physicians, and had spent all that she had, and was nothing bettered,

but rather grew worse,

27 When she had heard of Jesus, came in the press behind, and touched his garment.

28 For she said, If I may touch but his clothes, I shall be whole. 29 And straightway the fountain of her blood was dried

up; and she felt in *her* body that she was healed of that plague.

30 And Jesus, immediately knowing in himself that

virtue had gone out of him, turned him about in the press, and said, Who touched my clothes?
31 And his

disciples said unto him, Thou seest the multitude thronging thee, and sayest thou, Who touched me?

32 And he looked round about to see her that had done this thing.

33 But the woman fearing and trembling,

knowing what was done in her, came and fell down before him, and told him all the truth. 34 And he said unto her,

Daughter, thy faith hath made thee whole; go in peace, and be whole of thy plague.

35 While he yet spake, there

came from the ruler of the synagogue's *house certain* which said, Thy daughter is dead: why troublest thou the Master any further?

36 As soon as Jesus heard the word that was spoken, he saith unto the ruler of the synagogue, Be not afraid,

only believe. 37 And he suffered no man to follow him, save Peter, and James, and John the brother of James.

38 And he cometh to the house of the ruler of the synagogue, and seeth the tumult, and them that wept and wailed

greatly.

39 And when he was come in, he saith unto them, Why make ye this ado, and weep? the damsel is not

dead, but sleepeth.

40 And they laughed him to scorn. But when he had put them all out, he taketh the father and

the mother of the damsel, and them that were with him, and entereth in where the damsel was lying. 41 And he took the damsel by the hand, and said unto her, Talitha cumi; which is, being interpreted, Damsel, I say unto thee, arise.

42 And straightway the damsel arose, and walked; for she was *of the age of twelve years.* And they were astonished with

a great astonishment. 43 And he charged them straitly that no man should know it; and commanded that something should be given her to eat.

CHAPTER 6

AND he went out from thence,

and came into his own country; and his disciples follow him. 2 And when the sabbath day was come, he began to teach in the synagogue: and many hearing *him* were astonished, saying, From whence hath this *man* these things? and what wisdom *is* this which is given unto him, that even such mighty works are wrought by his hands?

3 Is not this the

carpenter, the son of Mary, the brother of James, and Joses, and of Juda, and Simon? and are not his sisters here with us?

And they were offended at him. 4 But Jesus said unto them, A prophet is not without honour, but in his own country, and among his own kin, and in his own house.

5 And he could there do no mighty work, save that he laid his hands upon a

few sick folk, and healed *them*. 6 And he marvelled because of their unbelief. And he went round about the villages, teaching.

7 And he called *unto him* the twelve, and began to send them forth by two and two;

and gave them power over unclean spirits; 8 And commanded them that they should take nothing for *their* journey, save a staff only; no scrip, no bread, no money in *their* purse:

9 But *be* shod with sandals; and not put on two

coats.

10 And he said unto them, In what place soever ye enter into an house, there abide till ye depart from that

place.

11 And whosoever shall not receive you, nor hear you, when ye depart thence, shake off the dust under

your feet for a testimony against them. Verily I say unto you, It shall be more tolerable for Sodom and Gomorrha in the day of judgment, than for that city.

12 And they went out, and preached that men should repent.

13 And they cast out many devils, and anointed with oil many that were sick, and healed *them*.

14 And king

Herod heard *of him;* (for his name was spread abroad:) and he said, That John the Baptist was risen from the dead, and therefore mighty works do shew forth themselves in him.

15 Others said, That it is Elias. And others said, That it is a

prophet, or as one of the prophets.

16 But when Herod heard *thereof*, he said, It is John, whom I beheaded: he is

risen from the dead.

17 For Herod himself had sent forth and laid hold upon John, and bound him in prison for

Herodias' sake, his brother Philip's wife: for he had married her.

18 For John had said unto Herod, It is not lawful

for thee to have thy brother's wife.

19 Therefore Herodias had a quarrel against him, and would have killed him;

but she could not:

20 For Herod feared John, knowing that he was a just man and an holy, and observed him;

and when he heard him, he did many things, and heard him gladly.

21 And when a convenient day was come, that

Herod on his birthday made a supper to his lords, high captains, and chief *estates* of Galilee;

22 And when

the daughter of
the said
Herodias came
in, and danced,
and pleased
Herod and them
that sat with
him, the king

said unto the damsel, Ask of me whatsoever thou wilt, and I will give *it* thee. 23 And he sware unto her, Whatsoever thou shalt ask of me, I will give *it* thee, unto the half of my kingdom.

24 And she went forth, and said unto her mother, What

shall I ask? And she said, The head of John the Baptist.

25 And she came in straightway with haste unto the

king, and asked, saying, I will that thou give me by and by in a charger the head of John the Baptist.

26 And the king

was exceeding sorry; *yet* for his oath's sake, and for their sakes which sat with him, he would not reject her. 27 And immediately the king sent an executioner, and commanded his head to be brought: and he went and beheaded him in the prison,

28 And brought his head in a charger, and gave it to the damsel: and the damsel gave it to her mother.

29 And when his disciples heard *of it*, they came and took up his corpse, and laid it in a tomb.

30 And the

apostles gathered themselves together unto Jesus, and told him all things, both what they had done, and what they had taught.

31 And he said unto them, Come ye yourselves apart into a desert place, and rest a while: for there

were many coming and going, and they had no leisure so much as to eat. 32 And they departed into a desert place by ship privately. 33 And the people saw them departing, and many knew him, and ran afoot thither out of all cities, and outwent them, and came together unto him.

34 And Jesus, when he came out, saw much people, and was

moved with compassion toward them, because they were as sheep not having a shepherd: and he began to teach them many things.

35 And when the day was now far spent, his disciples came unto him, and said, This is a

desert place, and now the time *is* far passed:

36 Send them away, that they may go into the country round about, and into

the villages, and buy themselves bread: for they have nothing to eat.

37 He answered and said unto them, Give ye

them to eat. And they say unto him, Shall we go and buy two hundred pennyworth of bread, and give them to eat?

38 He saith unto them, How many loaves have ye? go and see. And when they knew, they say, Five, and two fishes.

39 And he commanded them to make all sit down by companies upon the green grass.
40 And they sat down in ranks,

by hundreds, and by fifties.

41 And when he had taken the five loaves and the two fishes, he looked up to heaven, and

blessed, and brake the loaves, and gave *them* to his disciples to set before them; and the two fishes divided he among them all.

42 And they did all eat, and were filled.

43 And they took up twelve baskets full of the fragments, and of the fishes.

44 And they that did eat of the loaves were about five thousand men. 45 And straightway he constrained his

disciples to get into the ship, and to go to the other side before unto Bethsaida, while he sent away the people. 46 And when he had sent them away, he departed into a mountain to pray.

47 And when even was come, the ship was in

the midst of the sea, and he alone on the land.

48 And he saw them toiling in rowing; for the wind was contrary unto

them: and about the fourth watch of the night he cometh unto them, walking upon the sea, and would have passed by them.

49 But when they saw him walking upon the sea, they supposed it had been a spirit, and cried out:

50 For they all

saw him, and were troubled. And immediately he talked with them, and saith unto them, Be of good cheer: it is I; be not afraid.

51 And he went up unto them into the ship; and the wind ceased: and they were sore amazed in themselves

beyond measure, and wondered. 52 For they considered not *the miracle* of the loaves: for their heart was hardened.

53 And when they had passed over, they came into the land of Gennesaret, and drew to the shore.

54 And when

they were come out of the ship, straightway they knew him,

55 And ran through that whole region round about, and

began to carry about in beds those that were sick, where they heard he was.

56 And whithersoever he entered, into

villages, or cities, or country, they laid the sick in the streets, and besought him that they might touch if it were but the border of his garment: and as many as touched him were made whole.

CHAPTER 7

THEN came together unto him the Pharisees, and certain of the scribes, which came from Jerusalem.

2 And when they saw some of his disciples eat bread with defiled, that is to say, with unwashen, hands, they

found fault.
3 For the Pharisees, and all the Jews, except they wash *their* hands oft, eat not, holding the tradition of the

elders.

4 And *when they come* from the market, except they wash, they eat not. And many other things there be,

which they have received to hold, *as* the washing of cups, and pots, brasen vessels, and of tables.

5 Then the Pharisees and

scribes asked him, Why walk not thy disciples according to the tradition of the elders, but eat bread with unwashen hands?

6 He answered and said unto them, Well hath Esaias prophesied of you hypocrites, as it is written,

This people honoureth me with *their* lips, but their heart is far from me. 7 Howbeit in vain do they worship me, teaching *for* doctrines the commandments of men.

8 For laying aside the commandment of God, ye hold

the tradition of men, *as* the washing of pots and cups: and many other such like things ye do. 9 And he said unto them, Full well ye reject the commandment of God, that ye may keep your own tradition.

10 For Moses said, Honour thy father and thy

mother; and, Whoso curseth father or mother, let him die the death:

11 But ye say, If a man shall say to his father or

mother, *It is Corban, that is to say, a gift, by whatsoever thou mightest be profited by me; he shall be free.*
12 And ye

suffer him no more to do ought for his father or his mother;

13 Making the word of God of none effect

through your tradition, which ye have delivered: and many such like things do ye.

14 And when he had called all the

people *unto him,* he said unto them, Hearken unto me every one *of you,* and understand:
15 There is nothing from

without a man,
that entering
into him can
defile him: but
the things which
come out of
him, those are
they that defile

the man.

16 If any man have ears to hear, let him hear.

17 And when he was entered into the house from

the people, his disciples asked him concerning the parable.

18 And he saith unto them, Are ye so without understanding

also? Do ye not perceive, that whatsoever thing from without entereth into the man, *it* cannot defile him;

19 Because it

entereth not into his heart, but into the belly, and goeth out into the draught, purging all meats?

20 And he said,

That which cometh out of the man, that defileth the man. 21 For from within, out of the heart of men, proceed evil thoughts, adulteries, fornications, murders, 22 Thefts, covetousness, wickedness, deceit,

lasciviousness, an evil eye, blasphemy, pride, foolishness:
23 All these evil things come from within, and

defile the man. 24 And from thence he arose, and went into the borders of Tyre and Sidon, and entered into an house, and would have no man know *it*: but he could not be hid.

25 For a *certain* woman, whose young daughter had an unclean

spirit, heard of him, and came and fell at his feet:

26 The woman was a Greek, a Syrophenician by nation; and she

besought him that he would cast forth the devil out of her daughter.

27 But Jesus said unto her, Let the children

first be filled: for it is not meet to take the children's bread, and to cast *it* unto the dogs.

28 And she answered and

said unto him, Yes, Lord: yet the dogs under the table eat of the children's crumbs.

29 And he said unto her, For

this saying go thy way; the devil is gone out of thy daughter. 30 And when she was come to her house, she found the devil gone out, and her daughter laid upon the bed.

31 And again, departing from the coasts of Tyre and Sidon, he came unto

the sea of Galilee, through the midst of the coasts of Decapolis.

32 And they bring unto him one that was

deaf, and had an impediment in his speech; and they beseech him to put his hand upon him. 33 And he took him aside from the multitude, and put his fingers into his ears, and he spit, and touched his tongue;

34 And looking up to heaven, he

sighed, and saith unto him, Ephphatha, that is, Be opened. 35 And straightway his ears were opened, and the string of his tongue was loosed, and he spake plain.

36 And he charged them that they should tell no man: but

the more he charged them, so much the more a great deal they published *it*;

37 And were beyond measure astonished,

saying, He hath done all things well: he maketh both the deaf to hear, and the dumb to speak.

CHAPTER 8

IN those days the multitude being very great, and having nothing to eat, Jesus called his disciples *unto him*, and saith

unto them,
2 I have compassion on the multitude, because they have now been with me three days, and have

nothing to eat:
3 And if I send them away fasting to their own houses, they will faint by the way: for divers of them came

from far.
4 And his disciples answered him, From whence can a man satisfy these *men* with bread here in the

wilderness?

5 And he asked them, How many loaves have ye? And they said, Seven.

6 And he commanded the

people to sit down on the ground: and he took the seven loaves, and gave thanks, and brake, and gave to his disciples to set before *them;* and they did set *them* before the people.

7 And they had a few small fishes: and he

blessed, and commanded to set them also before *them*.

8 So they did eat, and were filled: and they took up of the

broken *meat* that was left seven baskets.

9 And they that had eaten were about four thousand: and he sent them away.

10 And straightway he entered into a ship with his disciples, and came into the parts of Dalmanutha.

11 And the Pharisees came forth, and began to question with him, seeking of him a sign from heaven, tempting him.

12 And he sighed deeply in his spirit, and saith, Why doth this generation seek after a sign? verily I say unto you, There shall

no sign be given unto this generation.
13 And he left them, and entering into the ship again departed to the

other side.

14 Now *the disciples* had forgotten to take bread, neither had they in the ship with them more than one

loaf.

15 And he charged them, saying, Take heed, beware of the leaven of the Pharisees, and *of* the leaven of

Herod.

16 And they reasoned among themselves, saying, *It is* because we have no bread.

17 And when

Jesus knew *it*, he saith unto them, Why reason ye, because ye have no bread? perceive ye not yet, neither understand?

have ye your heart yet hardened?

18 Having eyes, see ye not? and having ears, hear ye not? and do ye not

remember? 19 When I brake the five loaves among five thousand, how many baskets full of fragments took ye up? They say unto him, Twelve.

20 And when the seven among four thousand, how many baskets full of

fragments took ye up? And they said, Seven.

21 And he said unto them, How is it that ye do not understand?

22 And he

cometh to Bethsaida; and they bring a blind man unto him, and besought him to touch him.

23 And he took

the blind man by the hand, and led him out of the town; and when he had spit on his eyes, and put his hands upon him, he asked him if he saw ought.

24 And he looked up, and said, I see men as trees, walking.

25 After that he put *his* hands

again upon his eyes, and made him look up: and he was restored, and saw every man clearly.

26 And he sent him away to his

house, saying, Neither go into the town, nor tell *it* to any in the town.

27 And Jesus went out, and his disciples, into

the towns of Cæsarea Philippi: and by the way he asked his disciples, saying unto them, Whom do men say that I am?

28 And they answered, John the Baptist: but some *say*, Elias; and others, One of the prophets.

29 And he saith unto them, But

whom say ye that I am? And Peter answereth and saith unto him, Thou art the Christ.

30 And he charged them

that they should tell no man of him.

31 And he began to teach them, that the Son of man must suffer many

things, and be rejected of the elders, and *of* the chief priests, and scribes, and be killed, and after three days rise again.

32 And he spake that saying openly. And Peter took him, and began to rebuke him.
33 But when he had turned about

and looked on his disciples, he rebuked Peter, saying, Get thee behind me, Satan: for thou savourest not the things that be of

God, but the things that be of men.

34 And when he had called the people *unto him* with his disciples also, he said

unto them, Whosoever will come after me, let him deny himself, and take up his cross, and follow me. 35 For whosoever will save his life shall lose it; but whosoever shall lose his life for my sake and the gospel's, the same shall save it.

36 For what shall it profit a man, if he shall gain the whole world, and lose his own soul?

37 Or what shall

a man give in exchange for his soul? 38 Whosoever therefore shall be ashamed of me and of my words in this

adulterous and
sinful generation;
of him also shall
the Son of man
be ashamed,
when he cometh
in the glory of
his Father with

the holy angels.

CHAPTER 9

AND he said unto them, Verily I say unto you, That there

be some of them that stand here, which shall not taste of death, till they have seen the kingdom of God come with power.

2 And after six days Jesus taketh *with him* Peter, and James, and John, and leadeth them up into an high mountain apart

by themselves: and he was transfigured before them. 3 And his raiment became shining, exceeding white as snow; so as no fuller on earth can white them.

4 And there appeared unto them Elias with Moses: and they

were talking with Jesus.
 5 And Peter answered and said to Jesus, Master, it is good for us to be here: and let us make

three tabernacles; one for thee, and one for Moses, and one for Elias.

6 For he wist not what to say; for they were

sore afraid.
7 And there was a cloud that overshadowed them: and a voice came out of the cloud, saying, This is

my beloved Son: hear him.

8 And suddenly, when they had looked round about, they saw no man any more, save Jesus

only with themselves.
9 And as they came down from the mountain, he charged them that they should tell no man what

things they had seen, till the Son of man were risen from the dead.

10 And they kept that saying with themselves,

questioning one with another what the rising from the dead should mean.

11 And they asked him, saying, Why say

the scribes that Elias must first come?

12 And he answered and told them, Elias verily cometh first, and

restoreth all things; and how it is written of the Son of man, that he must suffer many things, and be set at nought.

13 But I say unto you, That Elias is indeed come, and they have done unto him whatsoever they listed, as it is written of him.

14 And when he came to *his* disciples, he saw a great multitude about them, and the scribes questioning with them.

15 And straightway all the people, when they beheld him, were greatly amazed, and running to *him* saluted him.

16 And he asked the scribes, What question ye with them?

17 And one of the multitude answered and

said, Master, I have brought unto thee my son, which hath a dumb spirit;

18 And wheresoever he taketh him, he

teareth him: and he foameth, and gnasheth with his teeth, and pineth away: and I spake to thy disciples that they should cast him out; and they could not. 19 He answereth him, and saith, O faithless generation, how long shall I be with you? how long shall I suffer you? bring him unto me. 20 And they brought him unto him: and when he saw him, straightway the spirit tare him; and he fell on the ground, and wallowed foaming.

21 And he asked his father,

How long is it ago since this came unto him? And he said, Of a child.

22 And ofttimes it hath cast him into the fire, and

into the waters,
to destroy him:
but if thou canst
do any thing,
have compassion
on us, and help
us.

23 Jesus said

unto him, If thou canst believe, all things *are* possible to him that believeth.

24 And straightway the

father of the child cried out, and said with tears, Lord, I believe; help thou mine unbelief.

25 When Jesus

saw that the people came running together, he rebuked the foul spirit, saying unto him, *Thou* dumb and deaf spirit, I charge thee, come out of him, and enter no more into him.

26 And *the spirit* cried, and rent him sore, and

came out of him: and he was as one dead; insomuch that many said, He is dead.

27 But Jesus took him by the

hand, and lifted him up; and he arose.

28 And when he was come into the house, his disciples asked him privately,

Why could not we cast him out? 29 And he said unto them, This kind can come forth by nothing, but by prayer and fasting.

30 And they departed thence, and passed through Galilee; and he would not that any man should know *it*.
31 For he

taught his disciples, and said unto them, The Son of man is delivered into the hands of men, and they shall kill him;

and after that he is killed, he shall rise the third day.

32 But they understood not that saying, and were afraid to

ask him.

33 And he came to Capernaum: and being in the house he asked them, What was it that ye disputed among

yourselves by the way?

34 But they held their peace: for by the way they had disputed among themselves, who

should be the greatest.

35 And he sat down, and called the twelve, and saith unto them, If any man desire to be first,

the same shall be last of all, and servant of all.

36 And he took a child, and set him in the midst of them: and when he had

taken him in his arms, he said unto them,

37 Whosoever shall receive one of such children in my name, receiveth me:

and whosoever shall receive me, receiveth not me, but him that sent me.

38 And John answered him, saying, Master,

we saw one casting out devils in thy name, and he followeth not us: and we forbad him, because he followeth not us.

39 But Jesus said, Forbid him not: for there is no man which shall do a miracle in my name, that can lightly speak evil

of me.

40 For he that is not against us is on our part.

41 For whosoever shall give you a cup of water to drink in

my name, because ye belong to Christ, verily I say unto you, he shall not lose his reward.

42 And whosoever shall

offend one of *these* little ones that believe in me, it is better for him that a millstone were hanged about his neck, and he were cast into the sea.

43 And if thy hand offend thee, cut it off: it is better for thee to enter into life maimed, than

having two hands to go into hell, into the fire that never shall be quenched: 44 Where their worm dieth not, and the fire is not quenched.

45 And if thy foot offend thee, cut it off: it is better for thee to enter halt into life, than having two feet to be

cast into hell, into the fire that never shall be quenched: 46 Where their worm dieth not, and the fire is not quenched.

47 And if thine eye offend thee, pluck it out: it is better for thee to enter into the kingdom of God with one eye, than having two

eyes to be cast into hell fire: 48 Where their worm dieth not, and the fire is not quenched. 49 For every one shall be salted with fire, and every sacrifice shall be salted with salt. 50 Salt *is* good: but if the salt have lost his saltness, wherewith will ye season it? Have salt in yourselves, and have peace one with another.

AND he arose from thence, and cometh into the coasts of Judæa by the farther side of Jordan: and the people resort unto him again; and, as he was wont, he taught them again.

2 And the Pharisees came to him, and asked him, Is it

lawful for a man to put away *his* wife? tempting him.

3 And he answered and said unto them, What did Moses

command you?

4 And they said, Moses suffered to write a bill of divorcement, and to put *her* away.

5 And Jesus

answered and said unto them, For the hardness of your heart he wrote you this precept.

6 But from the beginning of the

creation God made them male and female.
7 For this cause shall a man leave his father and mother, and cleave to his

wife;
8 And they twain shall be one flesh: so then they are no more twain, but one flesh.
9 What

therefore God hath joined together, let not man put asunder.

10 And in the house his disciples asked

him again of the same *matter*.

11 And he saith unto them, Whosoever shall put away his wife, and marry another,

committeth adultery against her.

12 And if a woman shall put away her husband, and be married to

another, she committeth adultery.

13 And they brought young children to him, that he should touch them: and

his disciples rebuked those that brought *them*.

14 But when Jesus saw *it*, he was much displeased, and

said unto them, Suffer the little children to come unto me, and forbid them not: for of such is the kingdom of God.

15 Verily I say unto you, Whosoever shall not receive the kingdom of God as a little child, he shall not enter therein.

16 And he took them up in his arms, put *his* hands upon them, and blessed them.

17 And when he was gone forth

into the way, there came one running, and kneeled to him, and asked him, Good Master, what shall I do that I may inherit eternal life?

18 And Jesus said unto him, Why callest thou me good? *there is* none good but one, *that is*, God.

19 Thou knowest the commandments, Do not commit adultery, Do not kill, Do not steal, Do not bear false witness,

Defraud not, Honour thy father and mother.

20 And he answered and said unto him, Master, all these

have I observed from my youth. 21 Then Jesus beholding him loved him, and said unto him, One thing thou lackest: go thy way, sell whatsoever thou hast, and give to the poor, and thou shalt have treasure in heaven: and come, take up the cross, and follow me.

22 And he was sad at that saying, and went away grieved: for he had great possessions.

23 And Jesus looked round about, and saith unto his disciples, How hardly shall they that have riches enter into the

kingdom of God!

24 And the disciples were astonished at his words. But Jesus answereth again, and saith unto

them, Children, how hard is it for them that trust in riches to enter into the kingdom of God!

25 It is easier

for a camel to go through the eye of a needle, than for a rich man to enter into the kingdom of God.

26 And they

were astonished out of measure, saying among themselves, Who then can be saved?

27 And Jesus looking upon

them saith, With men *it is* impossible, but not with God: for with God all things are possible.

28 Then Peter

began to say unto him, Lo, we have left all, and have followed thee.

29 And Jesus answered and said, Verily I say

unto you, There is no man that hath left house, or brethren, or sisters, or father, or mother, or wife, or children, or lands, for my sake, and the gospel's,

30 But he shall receive an hundredfold now in this time, houses, and brethren, and

sisters, and mothers, and children, and lands, with persecutions; and in the world to come eternal life.

31 But many *that are* first shall be last; and the last first.

32 And they were in the way going up to Jerusalem; and

Jesus went before them: and they were amazed; and as they followed, they were afraid. And he took again the twelve, and began to tell them what things should happen unto him,

33 *Saying,* Behold, we go up to Jerusalem;

and the Son of man shall be delivered unto the chief priests, and unto the scribes; and they shall condemn him to death, and shall deliver him to the Gentiles:

34 And they shall mock him, and shall scourge him, and shall spit upon him,

and shall kill him: and the third day he shall rise again.

35 And James and John, the sons of Zebedee, come unto him,

saying, Master, we would that thou shouldest do for us whatsoever we shall desire.

36 And he said unto them, What

would ye that I should do for you?

37 They said unto him, Grant unto us that we may sit, one on thy right hand,

and the other on thy left hand, in thy glory.

38 But Jesus said unto them, Ye know not what ye ask: can ye drink of the

cup that I drink of? and be baptized with the baptism that I am baptized with?

39 And they said unto him,

We can. And Jesus said unto them, Ye shall indeed drink of the cup that I drink of; and with the baptism that I am baptized withal shall ye be baptized:

40 But to sit on my right hand and on my left hand is not mine to give; but *it*

shall be given to them for whom it is prepared.

41 And when the ten heard *it*, they began to be much displeased with James and

John.

42 But Jesus called them *to him*, and saith unto them, Ye know that they which are accounted to

rule over the Gentiles exercise lordship over them; and their great ones exercise authority upon them.

43 But so shall it not be among you: but whosoever will be great among you, shall be your minister: 44 And

whosoever of you will be the chiefest, shall be servant of all.

45 For even the Son of man came not to be ministered unto,

but to minister, and to give his life a ransom for many.

46 And they came to Jericho: and as he went out of Jericho

with his disciples and a great number of people, blind Bartimæus, the son of Timæus, sat by the highway side begging.

47 And when he heard that it was Jesus of Nazareth, he began to cry out, and say, Jesus, *thou* Son of

David, have mercy on me. 48 And many charged him that he should hold his peace: but he cried the more a great deal, *Thou*

Son of David, have mercy on me.

49 And Jesus stood still, and commanded him to be called. And they call the

blind man, saying unto him, Be of good comfort, rise; he calleth thee.

50 And he, casting away his garment, rose,

and came to Jesus.

51 And Jesus answered and said unto him, What wilt thou that I should do unto thee? The

blind man said unto him, Lord, that I might receive my sight. 52 And Jesus said unto him, Go thy way; thy faith hath made thee whole. And immediately he received his sight, and followed Jesus in the way.

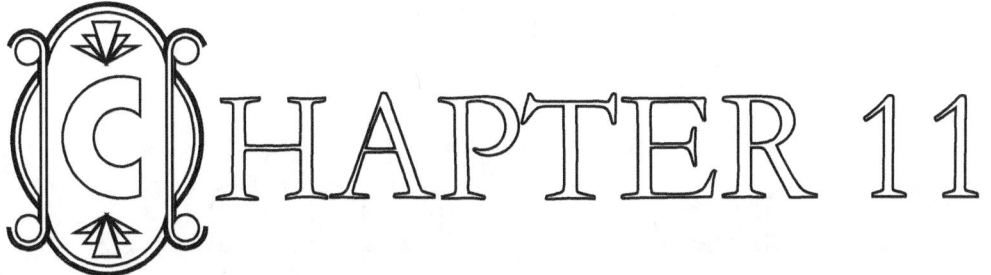
CHAPTER 11

AND when they came nigh to Jerusalem, unto Bethphage and Bethany, at the mount of Olives, he sendeth forth two of his disciples, 2 And saith unto them, Go your way into the village over against you: and as soon as ye be entered into it, ye shall find a colt tied, whereon never man sat; loose him, and bring *him.*

3 And if any

man say unto you, Why do ye this? say ye that the Lord hath need of him; and straightway he will send him hither.

4 And they went their way, and found the colt tied by the door without in a place where two ways met; and they loose him.

5 And certain of them that stood there said unto them, What do ye, loosing the colt?

6 And they said unto them even

as Jesus had commanded: and they let them go. 7 And they brought the colt to Jesus, and cast their garments on him; and he

sat upon him.
8 And many spread their garments in the way: and others cut down branches off the trees, and

strawed *them* in the way.

9 And they that went before, and they that followed, cried, saying, Hosanna; Blessed *is* he that

cometh in the name of the Lord:

10 Blessed *be* the kingdom of our father David, that cometh in the

name of the Lord: Hosanna in the highest.

11 And Jesus entered into Jerusalem, and into the temple: and when he had

looked round about upon all things, and now the eventide was come, he went out unto Bethany with the twelve.

12 And on the morrow, when they were come from Bethany, he was hungry:

13 And seeing a fig tree afar off having leaves, he

came, if haply he might find any thing thereon: and when he came to it, he found nothing but leaves; for the time of figs was not *yet*.

14 And Jesus answered and said unto it, No man eat fruit of thee hereafter for ever. And his disciples heard *it*.

15 And they come to Jerusalem: and Jesus went into the temple, and began to cast out them that sold and bought in

the temple, and overthrew the tables of the moneychangers, and the seats of them that sold doves;

16 And would

not suffer that any man should carry *any* vessel through the temple.

17 And he taught, saying unto them, Is it

not written, My house shall be called of all nations the house of prayer? but ye have made it a den of thieves.

18 And the scribes and chief priests heard *it*, and sought how they might destroy him: for they feared him, because all the

people was astonished at his doctrine.

19 And when even was come, he went out of the city.

20 And in the

morning, as they passed by, they saw the fig tree dried up from the roots.

21 And Peter calling to remembrance

saith unto him, Master, behold, the fig tree which thou cursedst is withered away. 22 And Jesus answering saith unto them, Have faith in God. 23 For verily I say unto you, That whosoever shall say unto this mountain, Be thou removed, and be thou cast into the sea; and shall not doubt in his heart, but shall believe that those things which he saith shall come to pass; he shall have whatsoever he saith.

24 Therefore I say unto you, What things soever ye desire,

when ye pray, believe that ye receive *them*, and ye shall have *them*.

25 And when ye stand praying, forgive, if ye

have ought against any: that your Father also which is in heaven may forgive you your trespasses.

26 But if ye do

not forgive, neither will your Father which is in heaven forgive your trespasses.

27 And they come again to Jerusalem: and as

he was walking in the temple, there come to him the chief priests, and the scribes, and the elders,

28 And say unto

him, By what authority doest thou these things? and who gave thee this authority to do these things?

29 And Jesus

answered and said unto them, I will also ask of you one question, and answer me, and I will tell you by what authority I do these things. 30 The baptism of John, was *it* from heaven, or of men? answer me.

31 And they reasoned with

themselves, saying, If we shall say, From heaven; he will say, Why then did ye not believe him? 32 But if we shall say, Of men; they feared the people: for all *men* counted John, that he was a prophet indeed.

33 And they

answered and said unto Jesus, We cannot tell. And Jesus answering saith unto them, Neither do I tell you by what authority I do these things.

CHAPTER 12

AND he began to speak unto them by

parables. A *certain* man planted a vineyard, and set an hedge about *it*, and digged *a place for* the winefat, and built a tower, and let it out to husbandmen, and went into a far country.

2 And at the season he sent to the husbandmen

a servant, that he might receive from the husbandmen of the fruit of the vineyard.

3 And they caught *him*, and

beat him, and sent *him* away empty.

4 And again he sent unto them another servant; and at him they cast stones, and

wounded *him* in the head, and sent *him* away shamefully handled.

5 And again he sent another; and him they killed,

and many others; beating some, and killing some. 6 Having yet therefore one son, his wellbeloved, he sent him also last unto them, saying, They will reverence my son.

7 But those husbandmen said among themselves, This

is the heir; come, let us kill him, and the inheritance shall be ours.

8 And they took him, and killed *him*, and cast *him*

out of the vineyard. 9 What shall therefore the lord of the vineyard do? he will come and destroy the husbandmen, and will give the vineyard unto others.

10 And have ye not read this scripture; The stone which the

builders rejected is become the head of the corner:

11 This was the Lord's doing, and it is marvellous in

our eyes?

12 And they sought to lay hold on him, but feared the people: for they knew that he had spoken the

parable against them: and they left him, and went their way. 13 And they send unto him certain of the Pharisees and of the Herodians, to catch him in *his* words.

14 And when they were come, they say unto him, Master, we know that thou

art true, and carest for no man: for thou regardest not the person of men, but teachest the way of God in truth: Is it lawful to give tribute to Cæsar, or not? 15 Shall we give, or shall we not give? But he, knowing their hypocrisy, said unto them, Why tempt ye me? bring me a penny, that I may see *it*.

16 And they brought *it*. And he saith unto them, Whose *is*

this image and superscription? And they said unto him, Cæsar's.

17 And Jesus answering said unto them,

Render to Cæsar the things that are Cæsar's, and to God the things that are God's. And they marvelled at him. 18 Then come unto him the Sadducees, which say there is no resurrection; and they asked him, saying,

19 Master,

Moses wrote unto us, If a man's brother die, and leave *his* wife *behind him*, and leave no children, that his brother should take his wife, and raise up seed unto his brother. 20 Now there were seven brethren: and the first took a wife, and dying left no seed. 21 And the second took her, and died, neither left he any seed: and the third likewise. 22 And the seven had her, and left no seed: last of all the woman died also.

23 In the resurrection therefore, when

they shall rise, whose wife shall she be of them? for the seven had her to wife. 24 And Jesus answering said unto them, Do ye not therefore err, because ye know not the scriptures, neither the power of God? 25 For when they shall rise from the dead, they neither marry, nor are given in marriage; but are as the angels which are in heaven.

26 And as touching the dead, that they rise: have ye not read in the book of Moses, how in the bush God spake unto him,

saying, I *am* the God of Abraham, and the God of Isaac, and the God of Jacob? 27 He is not the God of the dead, but the God of the living: ye therefore do greatly err.

28 And one of the scribes came, and having heard them reasoning

together, and perceiving that he had answered them well, asked him, Which is the first commandment of all?

29 And Jesus answered him, The first of all the commandments *is*, Hear, O Israel; The Lord our God is one

Lord:

30 And thou shalt love the Lord thy God with all thy heart, and with all thy soul, and with all thy

mind, and with all thy strength: this *is* the first commandment. 31 And the second *is* like, *namely* this, Thou shalt love thy neighbour as thyself. There is none other commandment greater than these.

32 And the scribe said unto

him, Well, Master, thou hast said the truth: for there is one God; and there is none other but he:

33 And to love

him with all the heart, and with all the understanding, and with all the soul, and with all the strength, and to love *his* neighbour as himself, is more than all whole burnt offerings and sacrifices.

34 And when Jesus saw that he answered

discreetly, he said unto him, Thou art not far from the kingdom of God. And no man after that durst ask him *any question.*

35 And Jesus answered and said, while he taught in the temple, How say the scribes that Christ is the Son

of David? 36 For David himself said by the Holy Ghost, The LORD said to my Lord, Sit thou on my right hand, till I make thine enemies thy footstool. 37 David therefore himself calleth him Lord; and whence is he *then* his son? And the common

people heard him gladly.
 38 And he said unto them in his doctrine, Beware of the scribes, which love to go in long clothing,

and *love* salutations in the marketplaces, 39 And the chief seats in the synagogues, and the uppermost rooms at feasts:

40 Which devour widows' houses, and for a pretence make long prayers: these shall receive greater damnation.

41 And Jesus sat over against the treasury, and beheld how the people cast money into the treasury: and many that were

rich cast in much.

42 And there came a certain poor widow, and she threw in two mites, which make a farthing.

43 And he called *unto him* his disciples, and saith unto them, Verily I say unto you, That this poor widow hath cast more in,

than all they which have cast into the treasury: 44 For all *they* did cast in of their abundance; but she of her want did cast in all that she had, *even* all her living.

CHAPTER 13

AND as he went out of the temple, one of

his disciples saith unto him, Master, see what manner of stones and what buildings *are here!* 2 And Jesus answering said unto him, Seest thou these great buildings? there shall not be left one stone upon another, that shall not be thrown down.

3 And as he sat upon the mount of Olives over against the temple, Peter and James and John and Andrew asked

him privately, 4 Tell us, when shall these things be? and what *shall be* the sign when all these things shall be fulfilled?

5 And Jesus answering them began to say, Take heed lest any *man* deceive you:

6 For many shall come in my

name, saying, I am *Christ;* and shall deceive many.

7 And when ye shall hear of wars and rumours of wars,

be ye not troubled: for *such things* must needs be; but the end *shall* not *be* yet.
8 For nation shall rise against nation, and

kingdom against kingdom: and there shall be earthquakes in divers places, and there shall be famines and troubles: these *are* the beginnings of sorrows.

9 But take heed to yourselves: for they shall deliver you up to councils; and in

the synagogues ye shall be beaten: and ye shall be brought before rulers and kings for my sake, for a testimony

against them.
 10 And the gospel must first be published among all nations.
 11 But when they shall lead

you, and deliver you up, take no thought beforehand what ye shall speak, neither do ye premeditate: but whatsoever shall be given you in that hour, that speak ye: for it is not ye that speak, but the Holy Ghost.

12 Now the brother shall

betray the brother to death, and the father the son; and children shall rise up against *their* parents, and shall cause them to be put to death.

13 And ye shall be hated of all *men* for my name's sake: but he that shall endure unto the

end, the same shall be saved.

14 But when ye shall see the abomination of desolation, spoken of by Daniel the

prophet, standing where it ought not, (let him that readeth understand,) then let them that be in Judæa flee to the mountains:

15 And let him that is on the housetop not go down into the house, neither enter *therein*, to take any thing

out of his house: 16 And let him that is in the field not turn back again for to take up his garment. 17 But woe to them that are with child, and to them that give suck in those days!

18 And pray ye that your flight be not in the

winter.

19 For *in* those days shall be affliction, such as was not from the beginning of the creation which God

created unto this time, neither shall be.

20 And except that the Lord had shortened those days, no flesh should be

saved: but for the elect's sake, whom he hath chosen, he hath shortened the days.

21 And then if any man shall say

to you, Lo, here *is* Christ; or, lo, *he is* there; believe *him* not: 22 For false Christs and false prophets shall rise, and shall shew signs and wonders, to seduce, if *it were* possible, even the elect.

23 But take ye heed: behold, I have foretold

you all things.

24 But in those days, after that tribulation, the sun shall be darkened, and the moon shall not give her

light,
 25 And the stars of heaven shall fall, and the powers that are in heaven shall be shaken.
 26 And then

shall they see the Son of man coming in the clouds with great power and glory. 27 And then shall he send his angels, and shall gather together his elect from the four winds, from the uttermost part of the earth to the uttermost part of heaven.

28 Now learn a parable of the fig tree; When her branch is yet tender, and putteth forth leaves, ye know that summer is

near:

29 So ye in like manner, when ye shall see these things come to pass, know that it is nigh, *even* at the doors.

30 Verily I say unto you, that this generation shall not pass, till all these things be done.

31 Heaven and earth shall pass

away: but my words shall not pass away.

32 But of that day and *that* hour knoweth no man, no, not the angels which are

in heaven, neither the Son, but the Father. 33 Take ye heed, watch and pray: for ye know not when the time is.

34 *For the Son of man is* as a man taking a far journey, who left his house, and gave authority to his servants, and to every man his

work, and commanded the porter to watch.

35 Watch ye therefore: for ye know not when the master of the house cometh, at

even, or at midnight, or at the cockcrowing, or in the morning:

36 Lest coming suddenly he find you sleeping.

37 And what I say unto you I say unto all, Watch.

CHAPTER 14

AFTER two

days was *the feast of* the passover, and of unleavened bread: and the chief priests and the scribes sought how they might take him by craft, and put *him* to death. 2 But they said, Not on the feast *day*, lest there be an uproar of the people.

3 And being in Bethany in the house of Simon the leper, as he sat at meat, there came a woman having an alabaster box of

ointment of spikenard very precious; and she brake the box, and poured *it* on his head.

4 And there were some that

had indignation within themselves, and said, Why was this waste of the ointment made? 5 For it might have been sold for more than three hundred pence, and have been given to the poor. And they murmured against her.

6 And Jesus

said, Let her alone; why trouble ye her? she hath wrought a good work on me.

7 For ye have the poor with

you always, and whensoever ye will ye may do them good: but me ye have not always.

8 She hath done what she could:

she is come aforehand to anoint my body to the burying. 9 Verily I say unto you, Wheresoever this gospel shall be preached throughout the whole world, *this* also that she hath done shall be spoken of for a memorial of her.

10 And Judas Iscariot, one of the twelve, went unto the chief priests, to betray him unto them. 11 And when they heard *it*,

they were glad, and promised to give him money. And he sought how he might conveniently betray him.
12 And the first

day of unleavened bread, when they killed the passover, his disciples said unto him, Where wilt thou that we go and prepare that thou mayest eat the passover? 13 And he sendeth forth two of his disciples, and saith unto them,

Go ye into the city, and there shall meet you a man bearing a pitcher of water: follow him.

14 And wheresoever he

shall go in, say ye to the goodman of the house, The Master saith, Where is the guestchamber, where I shall eat the passover with my disciples? 15 And he will shew you a large upper room furnished *and* prepared: there make ready for us.

16 And his disciples went forth, and came into the city, and found as he had said unto them:

and they made ready the passover.

17 And in the evening he cometh with the twelve.

18 And as they

sat and did eat, Jesus said, Verily I say unto you, One of you which eateth with me shall betray me.
19 And they

began to be sorrowful, and to say unto him one by one, *Is* it I? and another *said,* *Is* it I?

20 And he answered and

said unto them, *It is* one of the twelve, that dippeth with me in the dish.

21 The Son of man indeed goeth, as it is

written of him: but woe to that man by whom the Son of man is betrayed! good were it for that man if he had never been born.

22 And as they did eat, Jesus took bread, and blessed, and brake *it*, and gave to them, and said, Take, eat: this is my

body.

23 And he took the cup, and when he had given thanks, he gave *it* to them: and they all drank of it.

24 And he said unto them, This is my blood of the new testament, which is shed for many. 25 Verily I say unto you, I will

drink no more of the fruit of the vine, until that day that I drink it new in the kingdom of God.

26 And when

they had sung an hymn, they went out into the mount of Olives. 27 And Jesus saith unto them, All ye shall be offended because of me this night: for it is written, I will smite the shepherd, and the sheep shall be scattered. 28 But after that

I am risen, I will go before you into Galilee. 29 But Peter said unto him, Although all shall be offended, yet *will* not I.

30 And Jesus saith unto him, Verily I say unto thee, That this day, *even* in this night, before the cock crow twice,

thou shalt deny me thrice.

31 But he spake the more vehemently, If I should die with thee, I will not deny thee in any

wise. Likewise also said they all. 32 And they came to a place which was named Gethsemane: and he saith to his disciples, Sit ye here, while I shall pray.

33 And he taketh with him Peter and James and John, and began to be sore

amazed, and to be very heavy; 34 And saith unto them, My soul is exceeding sorrowful unto death: tarry ye here, and watch.

35 And he went forward a little, and fell on the ground, and prayed that, if it were possible, the hour might pass from him.

36 And he said, Abba, Father, all things *are* possible unto thee; take away this cup from me: nevertheless not what I will,

but what thou wilt.

37 And he cometh, and findeth them sleeping, and saith unto Peter, Simon, sleepest

thou? couldest not thou watch one hour? 38 Watch ye and pray, lest ye enter into temptation. The spirit truly *is* ready, but the flesh *is* weak.

39 And again he went away, and prayed, and spake the same words.

40 And when he

returned, he found them asleep again, (for their eyes were heavy,) neither wist they what to answer him.

41 And he

cometh the third time, and saith unto them, Sleep on now, and take *your* rest: it is enough, the hour is come; behold, the Son of man is betrayed into the hands of sinners.

42 Rise up, let us go; lo, he that betrayeth me is at hand.

43 And

immediately, while he yet spake, cometh Judas, one of the twelve, and with him a great multitude with swords and staves, from the chief priests and the scribes and the elders.

44 And he that betrayed him had given them a token, saying,

Whomsoever I shall kiss, that same is he; take him, and lead *him* away safely.

45 And as soon as he was come, he goeth

straightway to him, and saith, Master, master; and kissed him.

46 And they laid their hands on him, and took him.

47 And one of them that stood by drew a sword, and smote a servant of the high priest, and cut off his ear.

48 And Jesus

answered and said unto them, Are ye come out, as against a thief, with swords and *with* staves to take me?

49 I was daily

with you in the temple teaching, and ye took me not: but the scriptures must be fulfilled.

50 And they all forsook him, and

fled.

51 And there followed him a certain young man, having a linen cloth cast about *his* naked *body;* and the

young men laid hold on him:

52 And he left the linen cloth, and fled from them naked.

53 And they led Jesus away to the

high priest: and with him were assembled all the chief priests and the elders and the scribes.

54 And Peter followed him

afar off, even into the palace of the high priest: and he sat with the servants, and warmed himself at the fire.

55 And the chief priests and all the council sought for witness against Jesus to put him to death; and found none.

56 For many bare false witness against him, but their witness agreed not together.

57 And there arose certain,

and bare false witness against him, saying, 58 We heard him say, I will destroy this temple that is made with hands, and within three days I will build another made without hands. 59 But neither so did their witness agree together.

60 And the high priest stood up in the midst, and asked Jesus, saying, Answerest thou nothing? what *is*

it which these witness against thee?

61 But he held his peace, and answered nothing. Again the high priest

asked him, and said unto him, Art thou the Christ, the Son of the Blessed? 62 And Jesus said, I am: and ye shall see the

Son of man sitting on the right hand of power, and coming in the clouds of heaven.

63 Then the

high priest rent his clothes, and saith, What need we any further witnesses?

64 Ye have heard the blasphemy: what

think ye? And they all condemned him to be guilty of death.

65 And some began to spit on him, and to

cover his face, and to buffet him, and to say unto him, Prophesy: and the servants did strike him with the palms of their hands.

66 And as Peter was beneath in the palace, there cometh one of the maids of the high priest:

67 And when

she saw Peter warming himself, she looked upon him, and said, And thou also wast with Jesus of Nazareth. 68 But he denied, saying, I know not, neither understand I what thou sayest. And he went out into the porch; and the cock crew.

69 And a maid saw him again, and began to say to them that stood by, This is *one* of them.

70 And he

denied it again. And a little after, they that stood by said again to Peter, Surely thou art *one* of them: for thou art a Galilæan, and thy speech agreeth *thereto*.

71 But he began to curse and to swear, *saying*, I know not this man of whom ye speak.

72 And the second time the cock crew. And Peter called to mind the word that Jesus said unto him, Before the cock crow

twice, thou shalt deny me thrice. And when he thought thereon, he wept.

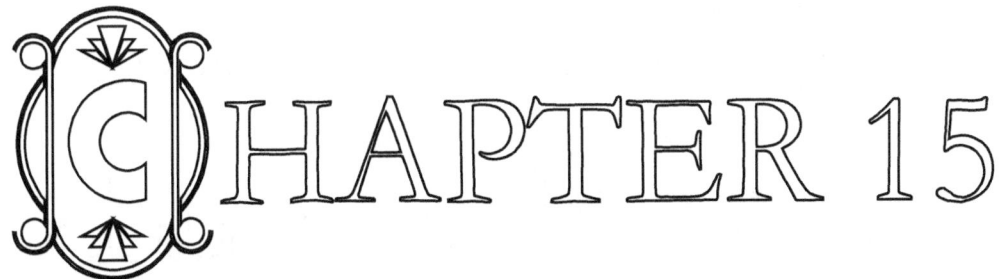HAPTER 15

AND straight-
way in the
morning the
chief priests held
a consultation
with the elders
and scribes and
the whole

council, and bound Jesus, and carried *him* away, and delivered *him* to Pilate.

2 And Pilate asked him, Art thou the King of

the Jews? And he answering said unto him, Thou sayest *it*.

3 And the chief priests accused him of many things: but he

answered nothing.
4 And Pilate asked him again, saying, Answerest thou nothing? behold how many things

they witness against thee. 5 But Jesus yet answered nothing; so that Pilate marvelled. 6 Now at *that* feast he released unto them one prisoner, whomsoever they desired.

7 And there was *one* named Barabbas, *which lay* bound with

them that had made insurrection with him, who had committed murder in the insurrection.
8 And the

multitude crying aloud began to desire *him to do* as he had ever done unto them.

9 But Pilate answered them, saying, Will ye

that I release unto you the King of the Jews?

10 For he knew that the chief priests had delivered him for

envy.

11 But the chief priests moved the people, that he should rather release Barabbas unto them.

12 And Pilate

answered and said again unto them, What will ye then that I shall do *unto him* whom ye call the King of the Jews?

13 And they cried out again, Crucify him.

14 Then Pilate said unto them, Why, what evil hath he done? And they cried

out the more exceedingly, Crucify him.

15 And *so* Pilate, willing to content the people, released Barabbas unto

them, and delivered Jesus, when he had scourged *him*, to be crucified.

16 And the soldiers led him away into the

hall, called Prætorium; and they call together the whole band. 17 And they clothed him with purple, and platted a crown of thorns, and put it about his *head,*

18 And began to salute him, Hail, King of the Jews!

19 And they

smote him on the head with a reed, and did spit upon him, and bowing *their* knees worshipped him. 20 And when they had mocked him, they took off the purple from him, and put his own clothes on him, and led him out to crucify him.

21 And they compel one Simon a Cyrenian, who passed by, coming out of the country, the father of

Alexander and Rufus, to bear his cross.

22 And they bring him unto the place Golgotha, which is, being

interpreted, The place of a skull.

23 And they gave him to drink wine mingled with myrrh: but he received *it* not.

24 And when they had crucified him, they parted his garments, casting lots upon them, what every man should take.

25 And it was the third hour, and they crucified him.
26 And the superscription of his accusation was written over,

THE KING OF THE JEWS.

27 And with him they crucify two thieves; the one on his right hand, and the other on his left.

28 And the scripture was fulfilled, which saith, And he was numbered with the transgressors. 29 And they

that passed by railed on him, wagging their heads, and saying, Ah, thou that destroyest the temple, and buildest *it* in three days, 30 Save thyself, and come down from the cross. 31 Likewise also the chief priests mocking said among themselves with the scribes, He saved others; himself he cannot save. 32 Let Christ the King of Israel descend now from the cross, that we may see and believe. And they that were crucified with him reviled him. 33 And when the sixth hour was come, there was darkness over the whole land until the ninth hour.

34 And at the ninth hour Jesus

cried with a loud voice, saying, Eloi, Eloi, lama sabachthani? which is, being interpreted, My God, my God, why hast thou forsaken me?

35 And some of them that stood by, when they heard *it*, said, Behold, he calleth Elias.

36 And one ran

and filled a spunge full of vinegar, and put *it* on a reed, and gave him to drink, saying, Let alone; let us see whether Elias will come to take him down. 37 And Jesus cried with a loud voice, and gave up the ghost. 38 And the veil of the temple

was rent in twain
from the top to
the bottom.
39 And when
the centurion,
which stood
over against him,
saw that he so

cried out, and gave up the ghost, he said, Truly this man was the Son of God.

40 There were also women

looking on afar off: among whom was Mary Magdalene, and Mary the mother of James the less and of Joses, and Salome;

41 (Who also, when he was in Galilee, followed him, and ministered unto him;) and many other women which came up

with him unto Jerusalem. 42 And now when the even was come, because it was the preparation, that is, the day before the sabbath, 43 Joseph of Arimathæa, an honourable counseller, which also waited for the kingdom of God, came, and went in boldly unto Pilate, and craved the body of Jesus.

44 And Pilate marvelled if he

were already dead: and calling *unto him* the centurion, he asked him whether he had been any while dead.

45 And when he knew *it* of the centurion, he gave the body to Joseph.

46 And he bought fine linen, and took

him down, and wrapped him in the linen, and laid him in a sepulchre which was hewn out of a rock, and rolled a stone unto the door of the sepulchre.

47 And Mary Magdalene and Mary *the mother* of Joses beheld where he was laid.

CHAPTER 16

AND when the sabbath was past, Mary Magdalene, and Mary the *mother* of James, and Salome, had bought sweet spices, that they might come and anoint him.

2 And very early in the morning

the first *day* of the week, they came unto the sepulchre at the rising of the sun.

3 And they said among themselves, Who

shall roll us away the stone from the door of the sepulchre?

4 And when they looked, they saw that the stone was rolled

away: for it was very great.

5 And entering into the sepulchre, they saw a young man sitting on the right side,

clothed in a long white garment; and they were affrighted.

6 And he saith unto them, Be not affrighted: Ye seek Jesus of

Nazareth, which was crucified: he is risen; he is not here: behold the place where they laid him.

7 But go your way, tell his

disciples and Peter that he goeth before you into Galilee: there shall ye see him, as he said unto you.

8 And they went

out quickly, and fled from the sepulchre; for they trembled and were amazed: neither said they any thing to any *man*;

for they were afraid.

9 Now when *Jesus* was risen early the first *day* of the week, he appeared first to Mary Magdalene,

out of whom he had cast seven devils.

10 *And* she went and told them that had been with him, as they mourned

and wept.

11 And they, when they had heard that he was alive, and had been seen of her, believed not.

12 After that he

appeared in another form unto two of them, as they walked, and went into the country.
13 And they

went and told *it* unto the residue: neither believed they them.

14 Afterward he appeared unto the eleven as they sat at meat,

and upbraided them with their unbelief and hardness of heart, because they believed not them which had seen him after he was risen.

15 And he said unto them, Go ye into all the world, and preach the gospel to every creature.

16 He that believeth and is baptized shall be saved; but he that believeth not shall be damned.
17 And these

signs shall follow them that believe; In my name shall they cast out devils; they shall speak with new tongues;

18 They shall take up serpents; and if they drink any deadly thing, it shall not hurt them; they shall lay hands on the sick, and they

shall recover.

19 So then after the Lord had spoken unto them, he was received up into heaven, and sat on the right

hand of God.
20 And they went forth, and preached every where, the Lord working with *them*, and confirming the

word with signs following. Amen.

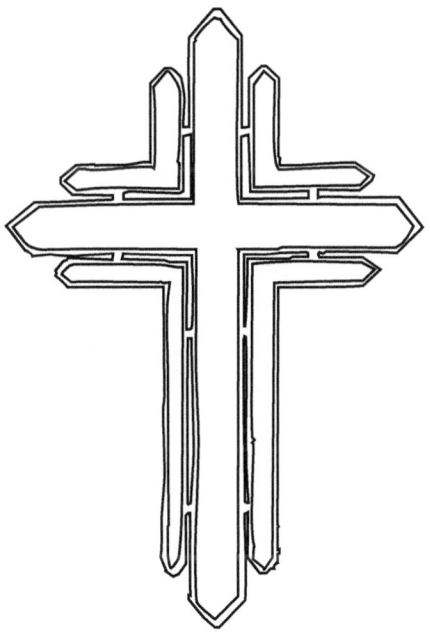

www.ingramcontent.com/pod-product-compliance
Lightning Source LLC
Chambersburg PA
CBHW080832230426
43665CB00021B/2815